The Storm Inside

AF624661

Kenya Mitchell

BookLeaf Publishing

Presentation by *BookLeaf Publishing*

Web: www.bookleafpub.com

E-mail: info@bookleafpub.com

ISBN: 9789357446051

First edition 2022

DEDICATION

I'd like to dedicate this book to all of the women that I have encountered and who have had a tremendous impact on me as a woman. We are strongest when we feel we are at our weakest. Thank you for being my example of strength.

ACKNOWLEDGE MENT

I'd like to thank you, the reader for taking the time to read this poetry book. I hope that it aids in helping you to not feel so alone, in helping you understand that we all feel because we're human and that in embracing our emotions, we keep a little of our humanity in a world that tries to strip that away.

Kissed

I've been kissed too many times
I remember the first time I was kissed
It was against my will, from then on it seemed
like all of the kisses that followed were like
trying to make up for lost time
Trying to get something that was already stolen
A moment of fireworks and weak knees
Never my testimony, I pray that should I
marry...My husband isn't disappointed with the
fact that a kiss with me is no longer sacred
I pray that my lips still have the ability to take
his breath away
I pray that I have the strength to trust in his
embrace and close my eyes, that Idon't have to
look for his response
I'll see it in his smile as we pull away and feel it
as he pulls me in for more

Good Bye

You played with my heart like a yo-yo. Still I'd rather be pulled back and forth like a tug of war than be without you. Though I know that I have to let you go because you keep proving that you can breatheproperly without me. That my absence isn't a knife to your heart and that you'd rather experience a life without me. That you're okay with missing me and not actually having me. It's crazy that I keep caressing your pride by reaching for you even though I find that it's bite is like poison to me. How stupid am I to think that you'd actually change? It's been six months, half a year and you're still okay. Well, I am not. I have to pull you name of out of my mouth disconnecting it from my heart, shutting down the love I once felt at the mere connection of our eyes. I have to bury the dream that was once my reality and I have admit that it hurts that you're no longer a part of me. I can clearly see that this hurts me more than it hurts you. I have to rest in peace knowing that my Father has me and He'll never stop loving me even though you have or even never did. I pray that you have a wonderful life. I pray that one day you recognize your loss for just that...your loss. That it teaches you to handle your good thing with care. I pray that she has the strength to endure you because I no longer have the predilection to lift you. This is good bye. Good Bye to a life we'll never share.

Mourning

The definition of mourning is the expression of deep sorrow for someone who has died, so it's hard to know how to feel about you because you're walking around breathing. I understand that you're grieving. I understand that you feel this is the end of our friendship. That you have to stay away from to better yourself. That I'm no longer allowed to be close to you. It hurts, but Iunderstand. I made this bed and although Yahweh is everywhere, I feel like I have to lay in the hell I created. Sorrow. It's burrowed so deeply into my heart that I feel it in my soul. I feel it behind my eyes when I look at you. I feel it in my arms that can no longer hug you. Sorry doesn't begin to explain what I feel for the death I've birthed between us. I want to be angry, blame someone else, but the verdict is on me. I'm guilty. I want to beg for mercy, what good will it do? Your mind's made up, you think the worst of me. I don't disagree. I just wish I could go back and fight myself for what I've done to us. I want so badly to actually communicate with you, somehow convey how much I don't want this to happen to us. We're supposed to be an enigma, this unexplainable example of

Yah-created connection. and I've ruined it. How do I not break down? How do I stop crying every night in mourning of what I no longer have? How do I stop you from hating me? Helplessly, I've tried to explain it to you. Tried to explain how I only tried to protect you. I can see it's gone in one ear and out of the other, refusing to stick. Even the truth seems to slip through my fingers, so I'm left empty. I wish I could make you smile again, make you genuinely feel the love I have for you. You've built an impenetrable wall, nothing will get through to you. I have to be okay with the way that things are. This is the normal now.

Here lies a beautiful friendship. I'd give anything to revive it, breathe life back into it, but I know that I can't. Maybe in the morning it'll be better. Whenever that may be.

Afraid

I'm sorry, I'm afraid to speak my truth because
when I do, you run.
It's like hearing I love you makes your heart race
and hands sweat.
Mouth dry with the revelation that someone
could possibly choose you. I see you.
I can't share hugs with you, you can barely
handle staring into my eyes without drawing
back into yourself.
It's like your body is already connected to mine
and your mind just refuses to comply. I know
you.
I'm afraid I'll never know what it's like to be in
your life because you don't even want to really
be alive. I can feel you pulling away from me
even now. I am you.

I'm Not Sorry

I'm not sorry anymore
I would run out of limbs for the number of times
I've said I was sorry and I really do mean it
In your eyes I hold the knife
You can't see that I stepped right in front of it
protecting you
I keep apologizing and still you're cold towards
me
Neither of us are victims here
I've apologized more to you than I have God
I know that putting up walls will only hurt me,
but I don't want you to be this close to me, close
enough to hurt me
I never meant for you to have so much power
over me
He said that I could trust you, but you're the one
who keeps hurting me
So I'm not sorry anymore
The guilt is not mine to carry anymore
Growing up can be scary, but pull up boot straps
because your war it's not with me
The second you really open your eyes you'll see
I've only ever wanted good for you
Yes, I've made mistakes
So have you

The reality is there's nothing I can do to change the way that you see me so I'm removing myself from the narrative.
I'm not sorry anymore.

Protected You

I protected your feelings because I'm so used to abusing my own. I didn't tell you that each time you pushed me away, a little part of me broke inside. Of course, it's not your fault, but who is really to blame? Is it me for thinking that just because He tied our lives together in heaven you'd automatically want me? That since He said yes, you'd want to say I do? Who is really to blame? Of course, not you. I protected your feelings, so you'll never know that I feel like your revolving door. You'll never know how badly you made me question my relationship, because at this point what is he really saying...this can't possibly be it. Yahweh never leaves you guessing. Of course, it's not your fault, but who really gets the blame because once you see this I'll automatically be the bad guy. I'll be the one to take the blame.
I protected your feelings, I thought love covered, now I'm choosing to pull back the sheets. Be the warmth for your own emotions. I'm done, I'm setting myself free.

Life

I don't enjoy much of anything anymore.
Like my lack of thirst for life is reminiscent of the guilt and regret I carry.
Like my brain has a silent conversation with my body about all of the bad things I've ever done.
I choke back the sobs I hold in at night, my pillow is very familiar with the taste of my tears and the weight of my sadness.
my chest aches with the things I wish I could do and those I wish I'd never thought to do.
Is this my punishment? Is this my reward? It tastes of rust and acid.
Shame. Embarrassment. They come back up in the memories I want so desperately to forget I ever experienced. I don't enjoy much of anything anymore.
Even breath is a reminder of how bad I am at the simplest of things.
A reminder that I don't do things right.
How I wish I could feel the relief of having done something right. Feel the flight of the high happiness provides.
Feel the warmth of the sun and inhale all of its promises.
Feel beautiful. Feel good. Fell like I'm enough.

I don't enjoy much of anything anymore, but I so desperately want to enjoy this life.

You

You feel like summer. Like the warmth of my favorite memory.
You heat my heart with the passion behind your eyes and ease in your smile.
When our hands connect, I feel it like an electrical current up my arm. You give me butterflies, that annoyinglyflap their wings inside my stomach. My palms sweat. Your mouth reminds me of smores. Sickeningly sweet, but you can't help going back for more. Your embrace feels like safety. Like it could protect me from the worst of storms and the darkest of nights, I easily rest in it.

The Audacity

The audacity. The Audacity to see my light and refuse to absorb it's warmth. The audacity to hold the hand of my emotions, but refuse to ever clasp your fingers with my own. The audacity. The audacity to fetishize my shape, but refuse to love my heart. The audacity to be so far away, but still want the benefits of being close.
I am worthy of love and all it's warmth. I am worthy of being appreciated. I am not stick figures or finger paintings. I am fine art, an exquisite masterpiece. Someone to be cherished and appreciated. Valued and treasured. And I'm audacious enough to know it.

Instability

There was a girl who never really had stability growing up. It seemed like she was always moving from place to place. By the time she started to make one friend or understand one lesson in school, it was time to pick up and move again. There was no stability in her relationships either. She watched her parents argue and scream at each other often, it got to the point that they forgot she was even in the room. 'Till this day, the poor thing still gets anxious when she hears people argue or any confrontation of any kind. It made her fear ever getting married, in fact, when she became a teenager she decided that if marriage meant yelling and leaving...she didn't want it. She didn't want love if it was going to hurt and all she knew was pain.

When the girl was about 5 years old, more instability came. This time it was in her mind and in her sexuality. Broken people don't have anything better to do than to break other people and so a broken person did their job. They touched her body and hurt her in a way that sometimes felt unreal. Bad things always seemed to happen to her in places that were supposed to feel like being in your Gran' Ma's bosom. They'd sit her on the changing table in the ladies bathroom at church and engrave into her tiny brain that being broken from the inside means you can hide it longer, like dust under a rug, you know it's there, but no one else knows except you. The broken person spun a web so tight around her that the little girl felt like she would suffocate from the pain. If she could've scratched her own skin off to get away from the pain, she would've. Except she couldn't. What about her siblings? The ones she was protecting and guarding against the shards of brokenness that had been slicing it's way through her soul. Stealing her innocence through drops of tears. When the girl turned 7 years old, the instability landed her family in a shelter and it was the worst thing to have to go through and even worse, when the girl turned 8 years old her daddy finally left her for good and whether the reasoning was legitimate or not...it hurt more that he didn't take her with him, even if it was just as unstable, even if she had to walk on the shards of brokenness to be with him. She had always had a connection with him, one that she never had with her mother and now she was being left with the one that she didn't know, one that she knew wouldn't protect her anymore than she had already. Funny how children are inclined to see what grown folks can't or won't see. They don't have a choice, they see even when they don't want to.

When the girl turned 10 years old, she realized that the broken shards weren't just in the girl's bathroom at church, they were in school too. They spoke nastily to her. Spoke to the insecurities that had been buried inside her chest before she was even thought of. It was like they had spit gasoline onto a burning house. The girl didn't understand why the broken shards drew back covered in her own blood. Couldn't understand why the world seemed to be covered in things that cut so deeply and seemed to walk over her as if she wasn't lying on the ground, barely alive, covered in blood.

When the girl turned fourteen years old, she realized the world was covered in glass. She had enough scars and newer open cuts to know that the world would never embrace her or keep her safe. She just knew that she had to forcibly remove herself from the hands made of broken glass. This would be the only thing that would save her from the pain. She no longer wanted to be alive, at least not like this and this was the only way she'd been accustomed to living. She

didn’t think that another kind of life existed. She didn't think it realistic to be hugged by life and feel the warmth of love and embers of trust. So she swallowed the very thing the brokenness had prescribed. She counted out 8 of them and flushed the rest down the toilet, she wouldn’t need them anymore...not that they worked in the first place.
Surprisingly, when she awoke the morning after, she was angry. Why wouldn’t she just stop breathing? Why didn’t the glass shard hands let her go?

At fifteen years old, She started thinking that maybe she’d just have to keep pretending that it didn’t hurt and that it didn’t bother her as much as it did. She tried to convince herself that she deserved this, she must’ve done something to upset the broken glass so much that they now wanted to put me away forever. Her mother sat her down and gave her the news that the glass was sending her away and she had two options, either go to the place all broken little girls go or go to the place where the broken ones are forgotten. She chose to live and hoped that one day, she’d find some stability.

Hate Me

I have a love hate relationship with movies. They both inspire me and tear me down. They give me the courage to be the me that I envision, but never cease to remind that this visual aid is nothing but a script, something conjured up by the writer's imagination. It's cruel and beautiful and sad… I see this beautiful, confident, fearless, woman in my head but that's exactly where she stays...my head. She doesn't come out, instead she leaves me to deal with my own insecurities and social awkwardness. In front of the world. I wish so badly that I could be her. Even if just for a day.

I want to be loved, to know what's it's like to see in someone's beautiful eyes that they are in love with me. I want to see someone look at me they was that guys look at girls when they fall in love with them in movies, see cruel reminder that movies aren't real. But can't I have a fairytale, dream come true? I know I'm far from deserving of one but just for a day couldn't I have a great career, one that I always enjoy, clothes and shoes that look like they came from a fashion magazine, friends who like me because they want to and not by default or force, and a guy who feels like he doesn't want to be with anyone else in the world except me. Success that makes those cruel reminders a thing to not concern myself with.

I wish I could be that minister, preacher that I envision. The one who everybody has no choice but to admire. You know, those people who make other people wish they had that kind of relationship with God. That preacher who is fearless.
I both hate and love fear. I hate it because it chokes me every single time I'm about to take a leap but I love it because it's been with me all of my life. It's consistent, I know exactly when it's going to come because it never misses an appointment, never fails to rear it's bold and ugly and terrible face. It never ceases to shut me up or shut me down. It's always there, frustrating me into giving up because "I'm no good at this anyway, right?"
I wish for just a day, I could be the fearless girl. The confident girl. The beautiful girl.

I don't like the girl I see when I look into the mirror, her skin is bad. Her hair never cooperates unless it's twisted, it no longer straightens. I hate that I see her big and fearful eyes looking back at me. Afraid to leave her job because "people" say it's where she's supposed to be. Miserable because she's stuck in this crowded and cramped shell of a person. So unsure about each and every step that she takes. Always imagining herself as a different person. A more beautiful person. A person worth being. I don't like that when I look at this girl she stares back at me like I'm supposed to tell her how to get out of this one and that one. Like I'm supposed to tell her that she's brave enough to say "hi" to that stranger. She just stares back at me and I hate, no I loathe that I am her.

Voice Like Fire

I try so very hard to speak with the gentleness of a lamb, but every time I open my mouth to speak it's like fire pours from my throat. I can feel my body cringe with discomfort as people's faces scrunch up with contempt for what I’m saying and the tone I'm using. I want so badly to not have such a hard voice and stone face. I cant turn it off and I certainly can control turning it on. Even simple statements sound like molten lava has been sitting in my mouth. Tongue destroying egos and motives all in one breath.

Anxiety

Anxiety, the weight of it presses down on my
chest like an elephant's foot.
It makes me question whether or not people
actually like me or if they just tolerate me.
It makes me cry in the middle of the night like a
child being torn from it's mother.
It snatches my breath and makes the room spin.
My mind races and none of my thoughts make
sense, I want so badly to crawl into a ball and
disappear.
Anxiety, you come up at the most inconvenient
times and you stop me from doing the things I'm
most afraid of, not for long though.

Stanger

I hate that strangers are walking around with my secrets. Carrying the essence of my past into their future. Carrying my tears along with their smiles. Taking with them my vulnerability and sensitivity. I hate that these strangers have familiar faces, but their eyes lack the warmth they once had. They no longer know me, no longer smile at me. To them, I'm just a stranger.

Maybe

I wish just for a moment that time would stop
Maybe that would put an end to my heart and mind racing to the death of me
maybe stop my disgust for me
maybe then the irrational thought and fears would stop harassing me
Maybe then I could smile without wondering if I'm celebrating too early
Maybe then the stinging behind my big brown eyes would stop before tears ever fell down my face as the evidence of my being in pain
Maybe then I could take a second to breathe
Maybe then I could have the courage to look at things in the dark.
Maybe

I am you

I sit in the seat next to you
I raise my hand in sync with your own
I lift my voice in agreement just like you
But I am not you, no
I am satan
I am Lucifer
I was once a bright star
So bright got a third of y'all, good look'n me
I am the itch in the back of your mind that tells you that you need something you can live without
I am greed
I influence you to look a little longer than you should, convince you in an award winning performance that surely touching isn't so like me
I am lust
Made you look at something that wasn't intended for the windows of your soul
I am deception
I persuade you to keep going against Him because He'll absolutely forgive you
I am that blinding rage that makes you forget reason and your mission for the remission of sinning
Don't I look just like you

I blind and blend in with the best of you so what does that really say about that the rest of you
I make you follow man like lost sheep, your shepherds are worse than you
I am suicide
I take your darkest stains you try to hide and tie them like a noose around the throat of your spirit, I watch as you fall to your knees
What? Can't hang man?
I am hatred
I am shame
Still thinking about what you did back when you were hooked? You just did
Got ya
I am guilt
I am fear
I know what keeps you from sleeping at night
I am not your brethren, I'll leave that to Raphael and 'em
He created us , but the relating stops there or does it?
I tricked Eve, what makes you think I have to do more than whisper in you ear to get you to bend for me
It is written that I wanted to be Him
You've got it all wrong
I wanted to be better
I am not your friend

I'll momentarily take away your loneliness and replace it with neediness or indifference or even a confusing combination of both. We'll call it asexual
I am pain
I am war
I am bloodshed
I am catastrophe
I am poverty
I am the government in God you trust
I am not a puppet
I am the master of things not real
I am Cain
I would kill you if I ever got the chance
I am not stupid
I am more shrewd than you'll ever get the opportunity to be
I know my role yet you so easily forget your own
I'm fine with being under your feet
Better to trip you there
Better you only see me as your shadow
You couldn't handle my true form
I hate red unless it's coming out of you
The only fork I have is to eat of your turmoil
A knife to cut away at your flesh, oh I love the taste of things that fester
A cup to drink the tears you shed
I am not light, no

I am darkness
I am death
I am the absence of His shine
I am you
Don't think so? Think about these words the next time you find yourself in bed with the likes of me

Falling in Love

Falling in love with you is like hearing music for the first time. You hear the song and then you listen to it again and again until the words are stuck in your head.. You don't realize it at first, but this song speaks words only your heart has whispered. It awakens something that connects your heart and soul. That's what it's like being in love with you. I hear and see your love for me on repeat and I never get tired of the words it speaks. It's my Stevie, Frank, India, Jill, Maxwell and everything in between. I promise to be the rhythm that calms you, empowers you to move forward and uplifts when you're down. I promise to keep our Heavenly father on repeat...drumming out the voices that aren't Him. I promise to keep Yah's voice as the foundation to this symphony.

Good

I got good at hiding pain behind a stretch of muscles in my face. I got good at hiding the tears behind the hours that everyone is asleep. I got good at making you feel like I'd chosen you over the other because let's be honest, I've gotten so good at pretending.

Memory

If I really sit and think about it, I'm more in love with your memory than I am with you. The thought of being with you causes my heart to ache and I know that I'd never be happy. I'd place myself in a box trying to protect you. I wouldn't be me and I've fought way too long to be anyone other than me.

Set me free

If you don't want me, set me free completely. Don't keep me around as a plan b or even to fill a seat for you. Find what or whoever it is you actually deem good because it's obviously not me.

Best for You

I want the best for you even if I am not the one causing the skin around your eyes to crinkle as the beginning signs of a smile. Even if I am not the one causing laughter and tears of joy, I want love to hold you just as warmly as I used to.

www.ingramcontent.com/pod-product-compliance
Lightning Source LLC
Chambersburg PA
CBHW051748130826
49812CB00033B/1047
* 9 7 8 9 3 5 7 4 4 6 0 5 1 *